Postcards from the Edge of Genius: Writing Your Way Through the World

Zach Sun

Published by Kento House, 2024.

POSTCARDS FROM THE EDGE OF GENIUS: WRITING YOUR WAY THROUGH THE WORLD

First edition. November 15, 2024.

ISBN: 979-8230891192

Written by Zach Sun.

Table of Contents

Table of Contents

To the explorers, the dreamers, and the storytellers—This book is for those who see the world not just as it is, but as it could be told.

And to the moments, both messy and magical, that make life worth writing about.

Epilogue: The Journey Continues

Writing about travel is like capturing starlight—fleeting moments of brilliance that shine long after the experience is over. As you embark on your own journey as a travel writer, remember that it's not just about the places you visit or the words you craft. It's about the connections you create—between yourself, the reader, and the world you're bringing to life.

From navigating the bustling seafood market in Birmingham to the quiet charm of Princes Street, this book has been a celebration of the unexpected moments that define our travels. Whether you find yourself haggling with a taxi driver in Istanbul or reflecting on the layered history of London's South Bank, each story you tell is an invitation to see the world through your eyes.

The tips and strategies shared in these pages are not rules but tools—guidelines to help you unlock your voice, structure your stories, and bring authenticity to your writing. Whether you're crafting your first blog post, pitching to a travel magazine, or building your brand as a writer, trust in your perspective. It's what makes your work unique.

Remember, great travel writing isn't about visiting every corner of the globe; it's about how deeply you experience the moments you do encounter. It's about the people you meet, the lessons you learn, and the stories that stay with you long after you've unpacked your suitcase.

And so, as you set out to write your next chapter—both in life and on the page—I leave you with this: every journey has a beginning, but the best ones never truly end. As long as there are new streets to wander, new faces to meet, and new stories to tell, your journey as a travel writer will continue.

The world is vast, and your words are the compass. Write bravely, explore deeply, and never stop searching for the edge of genius.

Introduction: Why This Book Matters

For over a decade, travel writing has been my passport to the world—a craft that has allowed me to translate fleeting moments into lasting impressions, immortalised in countless blogs, articles, and books. From the bustling markets of Bangkok to the quiet snowfields of Sapporo, I've had the privilege of sharing not just places but the essence of experiences with readers around the globe.

Now, I've taken on new assignments that will steer me in a different direction, at least for the foreseeable future. But before I hang up my pen, even temporarily, I want to leave behind something that captures the essence of what I've learned over the years. This book isn't just for you; it's also for me—a way to ensure that the techniques, insights, and lessons that have shaped my career don't fade into the rearview mirror of time.

Travel writing is more than a job or a hobby; it's a skill that can open doors, ignite dreams, and even pay the bills. It's not about simply describing a place—it's about taking your readers there, making them feel the cobblestones beneath their feet, smell the ocean air, or hear the distant hum of a city waking up. It's about finding the story that transforms a location into a living, breathing narrative.

In this book, I'll show you how to craft travel stories that are not only compelling but also marketable. You'll learn to blend vivid descriptions with cultural references, navigate the fine line between critique and praise, and build an authentic voice that resonates with readers. Whether you dream of writing for magazines, building a blog, or crafting your own travel book, this guide will equip you with the tools to succeed.

Travel writing isn't a dying art—it's evolving, just like the world itself. And while my journey is shifting gears, I hope this book inspires you to pick up the torch, pack your bags, and start writing your own.

Let's begin.

Kento House: kentohouse.com

Zach Sun's Patreon: patreon.com/zach_sun

Part 1: The Anatomy of a Compelling Travel Piece

Travel writing is more than just recounting an itinerary—it's an art form, one that requires a sharp eye, a curious mind, and the ability to transform moments into narratives that resonate with readers. When I first started writing, I thought the key was to simply describe what I saw: the sunsets, the landmarks, the bustling markets. But I quickly realised that what truly draws people into a story isn't the *what*—it's the *why*. Why should they care? Why does this place or experience matter, and what does it reveal about the world, or even about themselves?

The first part of this book focuses on the foundation of a compelling travel piece: the title, the opening line, and the overall structure. These elements are the scaffolding of your story—the invisible framework that holds everything together. Get these right, and you've already done half the work of captivating your audience.

Crafting the perfect title is an exercise in subtlety and precision, one that promises a journey without giving too much away. The opening line is where the story truly begins, plunging the reader into a world they can see, feel, and imagine. And then there's the structure—the flow of the narrative, the rise and fall of tension, and the rhythm that keeps the reader turning pages.

Each of these elements works together to create a story that feels alive, engaging, and worth reading. In this section, I'll show you how to master these techniques, using examples from my own writing and lessons learned from years of trial and error. Whether you're new to travel writing or looking to refine your craft, these chapters will give you the tools to start strong and keep your readers hooked.

Chapter 1: The Title That Hooks

A title in travel writing isn't just a label; it's the essence of the journey distilled into a few potent words. It's the moment where curiosity sparks and the reader decides whether they want to walk with you through your adventures. Over the years, I've learned that crafting a compelling title is an art of its own—a blend of intuition, storytelling, and a deep understanding of what makes a place resonate.

One of my favourite titles I've written came from a piece about my time in Kyoto: "Golden Afternoons at Kinkaku-ji." It was simple, elegant, and evocative—much like the temple itself. The title didn't need to shout or overpromise. It reflected the stillness of the gardens, the way the sunlight danced on the gilded surfaces, and the reverence of the moment. That's the kind of title that lingers with the reader, much like the experience lingered with me.

But finding the right title isn't always easy. I still cringe when I think about my early attempts, like "Exploring the Grand Palace in Bangkok." Accurate? Sure. Memorable? Hardly. It's the kind of title that disappears in a sea of travel articles. I had to learn how to dig deeper—how to capture not just the place, but the feeling, the story, and the invitation.

The Magic of Evocation

Titles that evoke emotion or curiosity are the ones that stand the test of time. Think about it: would you rather read an article titled "Riding the Shinkansen" or "Dreams on Rails: Japan's Bullet Train Adventures"? The former is a statement; the latter is an experience.

When I wrote about my journey from Tokyo to Hakodate on the Hokkaido Shinkansen, I wanted the title to reflect more than just the act of traveling. The train ride wasn't merely a way to get from point A to point B—it was a passage through misty landscapes, past snow-covered mountains, and into a world that felt both familiar and otherworldly. I ended up calling it "Through the Glass: Northern Japan in Motion." It captured the essence of gazing out of the train window, lost in the hypnotic blur of scenery.

The key is to focus on the sensory details that make a place come alive. For example, instead of saying, "The Beaches of Phuket," why not try something like, "Whispers of the Andaman: Phuket's Hidden Shores"? It's not just a title; it's an invitation to imagine the sound of waves, the salt in the air, and the quiet beauty of the moment.

Letting the Place Speak

Some of the best titles I've ever written came from listening to the places themselves. I still remember walking through Shinjuku at night, the neon signs glowing like modern lanterns in the drizzle. The sensory overload was overwhelming—in the best way—and I knew the title had to reflect that chaos and beauty. I settled on "Neon Nights in Tokyo: A Symphony of Chaos." It worked because it was rooted in the experience itself.

Another example came from a piece on the Old Quarter of Hanoi. I was struck by the way the streets seemed to hum with life—from the sizzle of street food to the chaotic dance of motorbikes. The title, "The Pulse of Hanoi: Life in the Old Quarter," captured the rhythm and energy of the city in just a few words.

Listening to a place means paying attention to its unique rhythms, contrasts, and quirks. A good title doesn't have to spell out every detail—it just needs to hint at the story, leaving enough mystery to draw readers in.

The Personal Connection

Your title should also reflect your personal connection to the place. When I wrote about the floating markets of Bangkok, I wanted the title to reflect not just the market itself, but the way it made me feel. I ended up calling it "Rowboats and Rituals: Bangkok's Floating Bazaar." It was as much about the people—the vendors who performed their daily rituals with quiet precision—as it was about the boats and the goods.

Personalising your titles doesn't mean turning them into memoirs. It means finding the angle that only you can bring to the story. What did you see, hear, or feel that others might overlook? What made the experience uniquely yours? When I wrote about the desert landscapes of Dubai, the title wasn't "A Trip to the Desert." It was "Shifting Sands: A Night in the Arabian Dunes." The title reflected not just the physical landscape, but the way it seemed to change with every passing moment.

Learning from Others

I've drawn inspiration from countless writers over the years, but I always make it my own. Take, for example, the titles you might find in *Lonely Planet* or *Condé Nast Traveler*. They're masters at crafting headlines that are both informative and enticing. A title like "Venice: Floating on History and Dreams" captures the romance of the city without resorting to clichés.

But inspiration doesn't mean imitation. I've learned to infuse my titles with my own voice and perspective. When I wrote about my time in Seoul, I didn't want to fall into the trap of generic phrases like "Modern Meets Traditional." Instead, I went with "Urban Hanbok: Seoul's Layers of Style," which reflected the city's blend of contemporary fashion and traditional Korean aesthetics.

Crafting the Perfect Hook

If there's one takeaway from my years of writing, it's this: a good title isn't just an accessory—it's the foundation. It's the first handshake, the first impression, and the first promise you make to your reader. So take your time with it. Play with words, experiment with imagery, and, above all, listen to the story you're trying to tell.

Because in the end, a great title isn't just about what it says—it's about what it makes the reader feel.

Chapter 2: The Opening Line

If a title is the door to your travel story, the opening line is the key that turns the lock. It's the moment where you either draw your reader into the scene or lose them to the noise of a thousand other distractions. Over the years, I've come to realise that a strong opening line is about much more than just setting the scene—it's about creating a sense of urgency, intrigue, and connection.

When I wrote about Kyoto's bamboo groves, my opening line wasn't "I walked through the bamboo forest." Sure, it described the action, but it didn't make you feel it. Instead, I wrote, "The bamboo swayed gently, whispering secrets I couldn't quite catch." It wasn't just about what I saw—it was about what I felt. And that feeling was the hook.

The Art of Immersion

The best opening lines are immersive. They drop the reader straight into the heart of the moment, bypassing introductions and pleasantries. Think about it—when you start a conversation with a story, you don't begin with, "Let me tell you about the time I was in Tokyo." You start with, "So there I was, caught in a sudden downpour in Shinjuku, with nothing but a flimsy umbrella between me and the neon-lit chaos."

It's the same with travel writing. Your opening line should make the reader feel like they've just stepped into the middle of something extraordinary. When I wrote about my time in Phuket, I began with, "The Andaman Sea shimmered like crushed emeralds, and I wondered how something so beautiful could feel so completely untouched." It wasn't about me—it was about the place, the moment, and the invitation to step into that world.

Sensory Details That Sing

One of the easiest ways to create an immersive opening line is to focus on sensory details. What did you see, hear, smell, taste, or feel? Start there.

When I wrote about Hong Kong's Victoria Peak, I didn't open with, "The view from the Peak is beautiful." That's an observation, not an experience. Instead, I wrote, "The city stretched out below me like a glittering web, each light a tiny heartbeat in Hong Kong's restless rhythm." The imagery was specific, evocative, and rooted in what I saw and felt at that moment.

Smell is another powerful tool. In Bangkok's Chatuchak Market, the first thing that hit me wasn't the sight of endless stalls or the sound of bargaining voices—it was the smell of grilled pork skewers, mingling with the faint tang of incense from a nearby shrine. So I started with that: "The air was thick with the scent of grilled pork and the soft bite of incense, a sensory handshake that promised both indulgence and tradition."

Asking Questions

Another technique I've found effective is to open with a question. Not a direct one like, "Have you ever been to Tokyo?"—that's lazy writing. Instead, ask a question that creates curiosity and invites the reader to think.

For example, when I wrote about visiting Sapporo's Snow Festival, I began with, "What compels thousands of people to stand in sub-zero temperatures, staring at ice sculptures that will melt into nothingness in weeks?" That question wasn't just rhetorical; it set the tone for the entire piece, exploring the fleeting beauty of the festival and the human desire to create art, even if it's temporary.

Starting with Conflict

Sometimes, the best way to draw readers in is to start with a challenge or conflict. When I wrote about navigating the streets of Istanbul, I didn't begin with a description of its storied history (though it's palpable). I started with, "The taxi driver quoted a price far above what the app displayed, his shrug leaving me with the unspoken rule of Istanbul: take it or leave it." That opening line captured the quiet tension of bargaining in a city where every interaction feels like part of the story, making the reader want to know how the experience unfolded.

Conflict doesn't always have to be dramatic. It can be something as simple as a misunderstanding or an unexpected twist. When I wrote about dining in a Michelin-starred sushi restaurant in Tokyo, my opening line was, "I didn't expect the sushi chef to laugh at me—but then again, I didn't expect to mispronounce 'uni' so badly that it sounded like 'rabbit.'"

Capturing Contrasts

Travel is often about contrasts—old and new, chaos and calm, tradition and modernity. Highlighting those contrasts can make for a compelling opening line.

When I wrote about Seoul's Gyeongbokgung Palace, I opened with, "Between glass skyscrapers and buzzing traffic, the palace felt like a whispered secret from a different time." That contrast between the city's modernity and the palace's history set the stage for a piece about Seoul's layered identity.

Similarly, when I wrote about exploring Singapore's hawker centres, I began with, "In a city obsessed with luxury, it's the plastic tables and $3 meals that hold its soul." That line wasn't just a description; it was a thesis statement for the entire piece.

Evolving My Style

When I first started travel writing, my opening lines were functional but uninspired. Over time, I realised that the opening line is your first chance to prove to the reader that the story is worth their time. It's not just about summarising where you are or what you're doing—it's about creating a moment that feels alive.

Now, I treat opening lines like poetry. Each word matters. Each image is deliberate. And I always ask myself: If I only had one sentence to tell this story, would this be the one?

The Rule of Revision

Here's a little secret: the best opening lines often come last. I almost never settle on my opening line until I've written the rest of the piece. Once the story is complete, I go back and find the moment, image, or idea that encapsulates everything I'm trying to say.

Sometimes, that means rewriting the opening line half a dozen times. But it's worth it. Because when you get it right, the opening line isn't just the start of the story—it's the moment where the reader decides to take the journey with you.

Chapter 3: Structuring the Flow

If the title is the door and the opening line is the key, then the structure of your travel story is the grand hallway that leads readers deeper into your world. A poorly organised piece is like a maze—disorienting and frustrating. But when done right, a well-structured travel story feels seamless, guiding readers through a narrative that unfolds naturally, each step building on the last. Over the years, I've come to see structure not as a rigid framework but as a dynamic dance, one that balances detail, emotion, and the rhythm of discovery.

Early in my career, I approached structure like a travel itinerary: chronological, predictable, and often dry. "I arrived here, I saw this, I ate that, and then I left." Functional, sure, but utterly forgettable. It wasn't until I started paying attention to the storytelling techniques in movies, novels, and even conversations with friends that I realised structure is about so much more than timelines. It's about moments—moments that resonate, surprise, and linger long after the story is over.

The Three-Act Journey

At the heart of any great travel piece lies the three-act structure, borrowed from the world of storytelling but perfectly suited to travel writing. Think of your story as a journey with three distinct phases:

Act One: Setting the Scene

The opening of your travel piece is your chance to establish the "why" of your story. Why are we here? What makes this place or experience worth exploring? This is where you introduce not just the location but the promise of the journey.

When I wrote about my trip to Kyoto, I didn't start with, "I visited Kinkaku-ji, the Golden Pavilion." Instead, I began with, "Kyoto, they say, is where Japan keeps its soul—and walking through the gates of Kinkaku-ji, I wondered if I was ready to meet it." This line didn't just set the scene; it introduced a sense of anticipation, a reason to keep reading.

To create a strong opening, lean into the details that make the location unique. Is it the history, the people, the food, or something less tangible, like the way the air feels or the way the light falls? In Bangkok, for example, it might be the chaotic rhythm of a tuk-tuk ride; in Tokyo, the quiet elegance of a tea ceremony. Whatever it is, let it shine in your opening.

Act Two: Diving into the Experience

The second act is where the magic happens. This is where you take your readers on the journey, immersing them in the sights, sounds, tastes, and emotions of the place. But here's the secret: it's not just about description—it's about connection.

Take, for example, my piece on Taipei's night markets. It wasn't enough to list the food stalls or describe the taste of stinky tofu. Instead, I wrote, "The smell hit me first—a sharp, fermented tang that made my nose wrinkle and my curiosity spike. Around me, locals lined up without hesitation, chatting as if the smell didn't exist. I hesitated, then took a bite, and the flavour was nothing like the smell: creamy, savoury, and completely unexpected."

Notice the progression: observation, reaction, interaction, reflection. Each step draws the reader deeper into the experience, making them feel like they're right there with you.

This is also the perfect place to weave in comparisons or alternative details. When I wrote about walking through Singapore's Gardens by the Bay, I compared it to New York's Central Park, but with a futuristic twist. "Where Central Park feels like an escape from the city, Gardens by the Bay feels like stepping into another dimension—a blend of nature and science fiction, where towering supertrees glow like something out of Avatar." Comparisons like this give readers a reference point while highlighting what makes the place unique.

Act Three: Reflecting and Concluding

The final act is where you bring everything together, leaving your readers with a lasting impression. This isn't the place for a generic summary—it's where you reflect on what the experience meant to you, what you learned, or how it changed your perspective.

When I wrote about visiting the Blue Mountains in Australia, my conclusion wasn't about the views or the hikes (although they were stunning). Instead, I focused on the feeling of standing at the edge of a cliff, looking out at the endless horizon. "The Blue Mountains didn't just show me beauty; they reminded me of the vastness of the world and my small but significant place in it. It was humbling and exhilarating all at once."

A strong conclusion often circles back to the promise you made in the opening. If you began with a question, answer it. If you started with a sensory detail, reflect on how it evolved. And don't be afraid to leave a little mystery. Sometimes, the best endings are the ones that linger in the reader's mind, inviting them to imagine the rest of the story.

Breaking the Rules (When It Works)

While the three-act structure is a great starting point, don't be afraid to break the rules if the story demands it. Some experiences are better told as vignettes—snapshots of moments that, together, create a larger picture. When I wrote about exploring Hong Kong's lesser-known neighbourhoods, I didn't follow a linear structure. Instead, I painted a series of scenes: the bustling wet market in Sham Shui Po, the quiet elegance of a tea house in Sheung Wan, the neon-lit chaos of Mong Kok. Each scene stood on its own but came together to tell a story about the city's contrasts.

The Rhythm of Discovery

Finally, remember that structure isn't just about where the story begins and ends—it's about the rhythm of discovery. Great travel writing mirrors the way we experience places in real life: moments of awe followed by moments of quiet reflection; bursts of action followed by pauses to take it all in.

Think of your story as a piece of music. The opening is the overture, introducing the themes and setting the tone. The middle is the symphony, full of crescendos and harmonies. And the ending is the final note, the one that echoes in the reader's mind long after the piece is over.

When I sit down to write, I don't think of structure as a constraint. I think of it as a framework for creativity—a way to guide readers through the story without ever letting them feel lost. Because in the end, the goal isn't just to tell a story—it's to make your readers feel like they've lived it.

Part 2: The Writer's Toolkit

Now that we've covered the art of crafting compelling titles, opening lines, and story structures, it's time to dive into the nuts and bolts of travel writing. Part 2 is all about the tools you'll need to transform raw experiences into stories that captivate, resonate, and, yes, sell.

I've always believed that travel writing is as much about the craft as it is about the journey. It's one thing to see the world; it's another to translate those sights, sounds, and feelings into words that transport your readers. This section is where I'll share the techniques and tricks I've refined over the years—the things that elevate good travel writing into something unforgettable.

Chapter 4: Descriptive Mastery

Chapter 4: Descriptive Mastery

Let me tell you a little secret: the best travel writers aren't just observers; they're interpreters. They don't simply describe what they see—they make you *feel* it. But mastering descriptive writing is a fine art. Overdo it, and you risk losing your reader in a sea of adjectives. Skimp on it, and your story falls flat. The key is to strike a balance, focusing on the details that matter most.

Painting with Words

When I was in Bangkok, walking through the Chatuchak Market, I could have described it as "a big, crowded market with lots of stalls." Technically true, but utterly lifeless. Instead, I wrote, "The air buzzed with a chaotic symphony of frying garlic, sizzling meat, and the sharp tang of lime. Vendors called out in rapid-fire Thai, their voices rising above the clatter of pots and pans, while shoppers elbowed their way through narrow aisles crammed with everything from antique jewellery to counterfeit sneakers."

Notice how I didn't try to describe *everything*. Instead, I focused on the sensory details—the smells, sounds, and textures—that made the experience come alive. The trick is to show, not tell. Don't just say a market was lively; let your readers *hear* the voices, *smell* the food, and *feel* the jostling crowds.

Choosing the Right Details

Great descriptions aren't about quantity; they're about quality. Think of your writing like a camera lens. You can zoom out to capture the big picture, or zoom in to focus on a single, striking detail. The key is knowing when to do which.

When I wrote about my visit to the temples of Angkor Wat, I could have easily gotten lost in the grandeur of it all. Instead, I zoomed in on a single image: "The roots of a towering banyan tree twisted around the crumbling stones, like veins clutching at the past." That one detail said more about the passage of time and the temple's history than any sweeping panorama ever could.

The Power of Metaphors

Metaphors are one of the most powerful tools in a travel writer's arsenal. They allow you to describe the indescribable, turning abstract ideas into vivid images.

For example, when I wrote about flying into Tokyo at night, I described the city as "a glittering circuit board, every light a pulse of electricity in a machine that never sleeps." That metaphor didn't just describe the view; it captured the energy and pace of the city itself.

But be careful—metaphors should enhance your writing, not distract from it. Avoid clichés like "a melting pot of cultures" or "a jewel of the East." Instead, strive for originality. Think about what the place *feels* like to you, and let your metaphors flow from there.

Balancing Description with Restraint

One of the biggest mistakes I see in travel writing is overloading the reader with details. It's tempting to describe every tree, every stone, every cloud—but remember, less is often more. Your goal isn't to recreate the entire scene; it's to evoke its essence.

When I wrote about visiting the Gardens by the Bay in Singapore, I didn't try to describe every plant or structure. Instead, I focused on a single moment: "As the sun dipped below the horizon, the supertrees lit up like sentinels from a sci-fi dream, their colours shifting from electric blue to deep magenta in a hypnotic dance."

By focusing on one vivid image, I was able to capture the mood of the place without overwhelming the reader.

Avoiding the Trap of Evaluation

Here's a hard truth: your readers don't care if you thought something was "amazing" or "beautiful." What they care about is *why* it mattered to you. Don't just tell them a place was great—show them. Let the details speak for themselves.

For instance, instead of saying, "The beaches of Phuket are beautiful," I wrote, "The sand felt like powdered sugar beneath my feet, while the Andaman Sea stretched out in a thousand shades of blue, each one brighter than the last." That description didn't need an evaluation—the beauty was self-evident.

Using Contrasts to Create Tension

One of my favourite techniques in descriptive writing is to highlight contrasts. Travel is often about juxtaposition—the old and the new, the natural and the man-made, the serene and the chaotic.

When I wrote about visiting the floating village of Kampong Phluk in Cambodia, I contrasted the stillness of the water with the vibrant life above it: "Beneath the stilted houses, the water lay still and glassy, reflecting the sky like a mirror. But above, the village bustled with life—children darting between wooden planks, women hanging laundry, and the faint hum of a distant motorboat breaking the silence."

By contrasting the calm of the water with the activity of the village, I was able to create a sense of tension that made the scene more dynamic.

Bringing It All Together

Descriptive mastery isn't about using the biggest words or the most flowery language. It's about choosing the right details, the right metaphors, and the right contrasts to bring your story to life. It's about making your readers feel like they're there with you, walking the same streets, smelling the same air, and experiencing the same wonder.

And the best part? Once you master the art of description, you'll start to see the world differently—not just as a traveller, but as a storyteller.

Chapter 5: Researching Like a Pro

Writing a great travel piece begins long before you set foot in a destination. It starts with research—not the dry, academic kind, but the kind that lights a spark in your imagination and gives you a deeper understanding of where you're going. In my early days of travel writing, I'd often skip this step, thinking I could rely on what I experienced in the moment. But I quickly learned that the best stories come from layering personal observations with historical, cultural, and even quirky details that only research can uncover.

The Art of Pre-Trip Research

Before I visit a destination, I dive into books, articles, documentaries, and even podcasts about the place. But I don't just focus on the obvious highlights or tourist attractions. I look for the stories beneath the surface—the lesser-known histories, the local legends, the cultural nuances that shape a place.

For instance, before my first trip to Kyoto, I stumbled across an article about the seasonal significance of moss in Japanese gardens. It wasn't something I'd ever thought about, but it gave me a whole new lens through which to view the city's temples and gardens. That detail made its way into my writing: "In Kyoto, even the moss tells a story, a living tapestry that shifts with the seasons, each shade of green a subtle reminder of time's quiet passage."

Research also helps you avoid clichés. How many times have you read about Paris as the "City of Light" or Bangkok as "chaotic but charming"? Digging deeper into a place's history, culture, and daily life gives you the material to write something fresh and original.

In-Destination Research

Once I'm on the ground, the research doesn't stop—it intensifies. I talk to locals, ask questions, and pay attention to the little details that guidebooks often miss. One of my favourite techniques is to ask open-ended questions. Instead of saying, "What's the best place to eat around here?" I'll ask, "Where do you go when you're celebrating something special?" or "What's a place you loved as a kid but rarely visit now?" These questions often lead to unexpected discoveries—hidden gems, personal stories, or unique angles that bring a destination to life.

During a trip to Istanbul, I struck up a conversation with a café owner who shared a story about the city's old tulip festivals, a tradition I'd never heard of despite hours of research. That conversation became the backbone of my article, with a title that practically wrote itself: "Istanbul in Bloom: The Forgotten Legacy of Tulips."

Balancing Research and Experience

Here's the tricky part: research is essential, but it should never overshadow your personal experience. Your story isn't just about the facts; it's about how those facts intersect with your journey.

When I wrote about exploring Singapore's Chinatown, my research gave me a deeper appreciation for the district's history, from the bustling opium dens of the 19th century to its modern revival as a cultural hotspot. But what made the story personal was the moment I stumbled upon a tiny herbal tea shop, tucked away in an alley, where an elderly woman insisted I try a bitter brew to "balance my chi." That blend of historical context and personal narrative is what makes a story compelling.

Using Unusual Sources

While guidebooks and travel blogs are useful, don't limit yourself to mainstream sources. Dig into academic papers, local newspapers, or even social media. Instagram hashtags, for example, can reveal trendy spots or hidden gems that traditional sources overlook.

When I was planning a trip to Seoul, I came across a Reddit thread about abandoned amusement parks in Korea. That led me to Yongma Land, a crumbling park that's become a favourite spot for photographers. The experience of exploring its eerie, overgrown rides became one of the highlights of my trip—and one of my most-read travel pieces.

The Role of Intuition

No amount of research can replace intuition. Sometimes, the best moments come from wandering aimlessly, following a hunch, or saying yes to something unexpected. Research gives you a foundation, but intuition is what turns a good trip into a great story.

In Istanbul, my guidebook pointed me to the Spice Bazaar, but it was my intuition that led me down a side street, where I found a tiny stall selling handmade soaps. The owner, an old man with a twinkle in his eye, told me he'd been running the stall for 40 years. That chance encounter became the heart of my story: "The Soapmaker of Istanbul: A Quiet Corner of the Spice Bazaar."

Organising Your Research

Once you've gathered your research, organise it in a way that makes it easy to refer back to later. I keep a digital notebook with sections for historical facts, cultural insights, and quirky tidbits. I also jot down my own impressions, thoughts, and questions as I travel.

This notebook becomes my treasure trove, a place where raw observations and researched details come together. When I sit down to write, I can pull from it to create stories that are rich, layered, and full of life.

The Secret to Great Travel Writing

The secret to great travel writing isn't just seeing the world—it's understanding it. Research helps you do that. It gives you the tools to dig deeper, to find the stories that others overlook, and to bring them to life in a way that feels authentic and meaningful.

So the next time you plan a trip, don't just pack your bags. Pack your curiosity, your questions, and your willingness to explore not just the place, but its stories. Because in the end, it's those stories that will make your writing unforgettable.

Chapter 6: Cultural Fluency in Writing

Travel writing isn't just about places; it's about the people, the traditions, and the unique cultural fabric that makes each destination stand apart. The best travel writers understand that to truly capture a place, you need to go beyond the surface. You need to speak the language—not just literally, but metaphorically. You need to weave in cultural references, local idioms, and historical context that make your story resonate deeply with readers.

When I first started out, I made the mistake of writing about destinations in isolation, as if they existed in a vacuum. I'd describe the streets of Paris without mentioning its storied history or the lingering shadows of its literary giants. I'd rave about Bangkok's floating markets without touching on their roots in Thailand's agricultural past. My writing wasn't bad, but it lacked depth. Once I started digging into the cultural context of the places I visited, my stories came alive in a way they never had before.

Why Cultural Fluency Matters

Travel isn't just about what you see—it's about how you understand what you see. When you write with cultural fluency, you invite readers to do the same. You give them the tools to see beyond the obvious, to appreciate the subtleties that make a place truly unique.

Take, for example, my visit to Tokyo's Asakusa district. Most travel articles would focus on the iconic Senso-ji Temple, with its bright red gates and bustling crowds. But I chose to focus on a quieter moment: watching a group of elderly women perform a traditional tea ceremony in a small teahouse nearby. It wasn't just about the tea; it was about the centuries-old ritual, the deliberate movements, and the sense of reverence that filled the room.

In my article, I wrote: "The tea wasn't just a drink—it was a conversation with history, a moment where the past and present met over a delicate porcelain cup." By framing the experience in its cultural context, I gave readers a deeper appreciation of what might otherwise have been just another cup of tea.

Using Cultural References Effectively

Cultural references are a powerful way to enrich your writing, but they need to be used thoughtfully. Too many, and your story risks becoming a history lecture. Too few, and you miss the chance to add depth and texture. The key is to weave them in naturally, like seasoning in a dish.

When I wrote about the vibrant chaos of Bangkok, I drew a parallel to the works of Wong Kar Wai, the Hong Kong filmmaker known for his dreamy, fragmented storytelling. "Bangkok," I wrote, "feels like a Wong Kar Wai film brought to life—colourful, chaotic, and full of fleeting moments that linger long after they're gone." That reference didn't just add flavour; it gave readers a new way to think about the city's energy.

To use cultural references effectively, ask yourself:

- **Is it relevant?** Does the reference enhance the reader's understanding of the place or experience?
- **Is it accessible?** Will most readers recognise the reference, or does it need a brief explanation?
- **Is it personal?** Does the reference reflect your unique perspective, or is it something anyone could have written?

Respecting the Culture You Write About

Cultural fluency isn't just about knowledge—it's about respect. When you write about another culture, you're stepping into someone else's story, and it's important to handle that responsibility with care. Avoid stereotypes, overgeneralisations, and the kind of shallow observations that reduce a culture to a set of clichés.

For example, when I wrote about Bali, I didn't describe it as "a tropical paradise"—a phrase so overused it's practically meaningless. Instead, I focused on the intricate beauty of the island's offerings: the rhythmic chanting of a temple ceremony, the vibrant colours of a Balinese dance, and the way locals weave spirituality into their everyday lives.

I also made a point to acknowledge my position as an outsider. In one piece, I wrote: "As a visitor, I could only glimpse the surface of Bali's deep spiritual traditions, but even that glimpse was enough to leave me humbled and inspired." This kind of humility goes a long way in showing readers—and the people you're writing about—that you understand the limits of your perspective.

Learning the Local Language

One of the easiest ways to show cultural fluency is to sprinkle in a few words or phrases from the local language. But be careful—context matters. Using local terms without understanding their deeper significance can come across as superficial or even disrespectful.

If you're not fluent in the language, focus on words or phrases that add meaning to your story. And always double-check your usage—there's nothing worse than using a word incorrectly and losing your readers' trust.

Cultural Fluency Through Observation

Sometimes, cultural fluency comes not from research or language, but from simply paying attention. I remember sitting in a café in Paris, watching locals sip their coffee with a leisurely air that felt worlds apart from the rush of an American Starbucks. That moment became the opening of my article, where I wrote: "In Paris, coffee isn't just a drink—it's a ritual, a pause, a quiet rebellion against the tyranny of time."

By observing the small details—the way people interacted, the pace of life, the unspoken rules of social etiquette—I was able to capture something authentic about Parisian culture.

Bringing Cultural Context to Life

Great travel writing doesn't just describe a place; it connects it to the larger world. When I wrote about visiting the Alhambra in Spain, I didn't just describe the intricate tilework or the stunning views of Granada. I talked about the Moorish influence on Spanish architecture, the blending of Islamic and Christian traditions, and how those cultural layers still shape Andalusia today.

This kind of context adds richness to your story, helping readers see the destination not just as a place, but as a living, breathing part of history and culture.

The Beauty of Nuance

Cultural fluency is about embracing nuance—the grey areas, the contradictions, and the things that can't be easily categorised. It's about understanding that every place, every culture, is more than the sum of its parts.

In the end, writing with cultural fluency isn't just about doing your homework. It's about being curious, empathetic, and willing to see the world through someone else's eyes. And when you bring that perspective to your writing, you create stories that resonate not just with your readers, but with the people and places you're writing about.

Part 3: Writing for Different Audiences

Travel writing is a conversation, a bridge between your experiences and the expectations of your readers. To connect with your audience, you need to craft your stories with them in mind—whether they're Gen Z adventurers seeking quirky escapades or middle-aged readers who value refined, meaningful experiences. Over time, I've learned that every audience craves authenticity; it's how you present that authenticity that changes depending on who you're speaking to.

Chapter 7: The Age Gap Between Audiences

When I write about places I've been, I tailor my lens to the essence of the experience. Sometimes it's the lively energy of a market, other times it's a quiet corner with unexpected charm. By knowing my audience and my own voice, I strike the balance between storytelling and resonance.

Writing for Gen Z

Let's begin with Gen Z—the social media-savvy, meme-sharing crowd that looks for vibrant, authentic, and visually stimulating experiences. To reach them, you need to write with immediacy and a sense of playfulness, focusing on moments that feel as real as they are captivating.

Take, for example, my visit to Birmingham's seafood market. It wasn't just a place to buy fish; it was an explosion of life, smell, and sound. "The scent of fresh oysters and sizzling prawns lingered in the air, mingling with the boisterous laughter of traders shouting out the day's deals. A lady with a floral apron handed me a bag of cockles with a grin that said, 'This is Birmingham—welcome to the heart of it.'"

Gen Z loves experiences that feel alive and relatable, so I let the scene do the talking. Details like the apron, the grin, and the sensory overload make the market feel immediate and tangible.

Humour also resonates with younger readers. For instance, when I wrote about the London Eye, I added a self-deprecating touch: "Somewhere between the fifth selfie and my failed attempt to look nonchalant at 443 feet, I realised the real charm of the Eye isn't the view—it's the excuse to feel like a kid on a Ferris wheel again."

Appealing to Middle-Aged Readers

Middle-aged readers often look for depth and reflection in travel writing. They want stories that offer context and meaning, something that connects the moment to a larger narrative. For this audience, I lean into the history, culture, and nuance of the places I visit.

When I wrote about Princes Street in Edinburgh, I focused on its unique mix of urban energy and natural beauty: "Princes Street is a promenade of contrasts—on one side, the bustling shops and cafés hum with modern life; on the other, the serene expanse of Princes Street Gardens offers a moment of calm, with the Edinburgh Castle standing watch in the distance like a silent guardian of the city's past."

This kind of writing isn't about showing off—it's about creating an emotional connection. By weaving in historical references and a sense of place, I invite readers to imagine themselves there, soaking up the atmosphere.

Even in London, where I typically avoid museums, there's something evocative about the Freud Museum that's worth noting. "The Freud Museum isn't just a house; it's a snapshot of a mind that shaped modern thought. Walking through his study, you can almost hear the whispers of psychoanalysis, the echoes of a man who dissected the human psyche with the precision of a surgeon." For middle-aged readers, these details offer depth and a touch of intellectual curiosity.

Bridging the Gap Between Audiences

Balancing the needs of younger and older readers might seem daunting, but it's surprisingly natural when you focus on shared experiences. For instance, when I wrote about London's South Bank, I combined elements that appealed to both.

For Gen Z, I highlighted the energy: "Street performers turned the riverside into a stage, their antics drawing crowds as the golden glow of the setting sun bathed the Thames in light." For middle-aged readers, I added a reflective layer: "The South Bank feels like a meeting point of old and new, where the historic arches of the bridges frame a city that's constantly reinventing itself."

This dual approach doesn't dilute the story—it enriches it, offering multiple entry points for readers with different tastes.

Tone and Style: Shifting the Lens

Tone is the secret to tailoring your writing. For younger readers, I might use a conversational and irreverent style: "If you're in Edinburgh and don't stop for a photo at the Scott Monument, don't worry—Instagram will remind you you're missing out." For older readers, I'd adopt a more polished, contemplative tone: "The Scott Monument stands as a testament to Edinburgh's literary heritage, its gothic spires a reminder of the city's devotion to the written word."

Both styles convey the same information, but they speak to different sensibilities. It's like capturing the same view through two different lenses—each one highlighting something unique.

Avoiding Stereotypes

The key to writing for any audience is to avoid pigeonholing them into predictable stereotypes. Not every Gen Z reader wants quirky anecdotes, and not every middle-aged reader cares about historical context. People are complex, and great travel writing reflects that complexity.

When I wrote about London's Borough Market, I didn't focus solely on its Instagrammable corners or its foodie credentials. Instead, I highlighted its layers: "The market is a tapestry of smells and stories, where the aroma of fresh bread mingles with the chatter of traders who've been here for decades. It's a place where history and gastronomy collide, each bite a taste of London's multicultural soul."

By embracing both the market's energy and its legacy, I created a story that appealed to a wide range of readers.

Universal Connection

At its heart, travel writing is about creating a connection—between you and your readers, between the reader and the place. Whether you're writing for a Gen Z adventurer or a middle-aged dreamer, the goal is to make them feel something: curiosity, nostalgia, inspiration.

The best stories transcend demographics. They remind us that no matter where we come from or what we seek, there's something universal in the act of exploring the world.

Chapter 8: Navigating Controversy Gracefully

Travel writing has the power to connect cultures, spark wanderlust, and celebrate the beauty of the world—but it can also touch on uncomfortable truths. Destinations aren't isolated from the complexities of history, politics, and social dynamics, and ignoring these elements can make your writing feel shallow or disconnected. At the same time, tackling controversy head-on requires finesse. Done poorly, it can alienate readers or come across as judgmental.

Over the years, I've learned that the key to navigating controversy in travel writing is to approach it with curiosity, empathy, and nuance. It's not about avoiding difficult topics—it's about framing them in a way that invites reflection rather than defensiveness.

Acknowledging the Layers

Every destination has its contradictions. London, for instance, is a city of dazzling wealth and undeniable inequality, where five-star hotels share streets with unhoused people seeking shelter. Ignoring these contrasts feels dishonest, but addressing them too bluntly can overshadow the story you're trying to tell.

When I wrote about my walk along the South Bank, I chose to weave these layers into the narrative subtly: "The golden light of the Thames at sunset hides nothing—the gleam of the Shard reflecting the city's ambition, the quiet shadows of those left behind in its wake. London's charm lies in its complexity, its refusal to be simplified." This approach acknowledges the disparity without letting it dominate the piece.

Using Observation, Not Opinion

One of the best ways to tackle controversial topics is to let the scene speak for itself. Instead of delivering a verdict, describe what you see and allow readers to draw their own conclusions.

For example, during a visit to Bangkok, I noticed the stark contrast between the city's luxurious malls and the humble street stalls just a few steps away. Instead of critiquing this outright, I wrote: "Inside the air-conditioned glow of Siam Paragon, designer handbags gleamed under perfect lighting. Outside, a woman stirred a bubbling pot of noodles over a charcoal stove, her hands moving with practiced efficiency. The two worlds existed side by side, each as much a part of Bangkok as the other."

By focusing on observation, you can highlight disparities or contradictions without sounding preachy or judgmental.

Framing Controversy Through Personal Experience

Sometimes, the best way to address a difficult topic is through your own perspective. Share how it made you feel, what questions it raised, or how it changed your understanding of the place.

When I visited Princes Street in Edinburgh, I was struck by the tension between its commercial bustle and the quiet beauty of the gardens below. I wrote: "Walking along Princes Street, I felt torn between two worlds—the hurried pace of shoppers rushing past and the serene stillness of the gardens below, where time seemed to pause. It made me wonder: Do we ever truly pause, or are we always rushing to the next thing?"

This reflective approach allows you to engage with controversial or thought-provoking themes without assigning blame or oversimplifying the issue.

Using Historical Context

History often provides a lens through which to explore controversial topics. By grounding your observations in historical facts, you can add depth to your writing and help readers see the bigger picture.

For instance, when I wrote about the Freud Museum in London, I didn't shy away from the complexities of Freud's legacy. Instead, I framed it within the broader context of psychoanalysis: "Freud's study, with its shelves of ancient artefacts, feels like a time capsule—a room where ideas that reshaped the world were born. Yet, his theories remain as debated as they are celebrated, a reminder that no legacy is without its shadows."

This approach acknowledges controversy while showing respect for the subject's significance.

Humour as a Buffer

Humour can be a powerful tool for addressing controversy without alienating your audience. A touch of irony or self-deprecation can defuse tension and invite readers to engage with difficult topics in a more relaxed way.

During a visit to Birmingham's seafood market, I noticed the unapologetic bluntness of the traders. Instead of criticising it, I embraced the humour: "If you're looking for customer service with a smile, you won't find it here. But if you want the freshest crab in the city, you'd better learn to shout louder than the guy next to you."

Humour doesn't trivialise the subject—it humanises it, making it easier for readers to engage with.

Giving a Voice to Others

One of the most respectful ways to navigate controversy is to let others speak for themselves. Including quotes or anecdotes from locals can provide a perspective that's grounded in lived experience, rather than your own interpretation.

When I wrote about the changing face of London's markets, I included a conversation with a vendor: "We've seen it all," she told me, her hands deftly packing fresh prawns. "Gentrification's good for business, sure, but sometimes I miss the old days when it was rougher. More real, you know?"

By including her voice, I added authenticity to the piece and avoided speaking on behalf of others.

Ending on a Thoughtful Note

When addressing controversy, it's important to leave readers with something to ponder—a question, a reflection, or an invitation to think differently.

In one piece about London's gentrification, I concluded with: "Cities, like people, are always changing. The question is, who gets to decide what they become—and who gets left behind in the process?" This kind of ending doesn't offer easy answers, but it encourages readers to engage with the topic long after they've finished the article.

The Balancing Act

Navigating controversy in travel writing is a balancing act. It's about being honest without being divisive, reflective without being heavy-handed. It's about showing respect for the places and people you write about, while also challenging your readers to see the world in a new way.

Because travel isn't always comfortable. It's not always easy or beautiful. But it is always worth writing about.

Part 4: Building Authority as a Travel Writer

Travel writing is more than just sharing your journeys—it's about establishing yourself as an authority in a crowded field. Authority isn't something you claim; it's something you earn through consistent, high-quality work that resonates with readers and builds trust. This section is all about turning your passion for travel writing into a platform that not only inspires but also opens doors to new opportunities, income streams, and influence.

Chapter 9: Creating a Portfolio

When I first started travel writing, the idea of creating a portfolio felt overwhelming. How do you even begin to showcase your work when you're just starting out? What should you include? Who are you even creating it for? Over the years, I've realised that building a portfolio isn't about quantity; it's about curating pieces that showcase your voice, your perspective, and your ability to tell a story that resonates.

A strong portfolio is more than just a collection of articles or blog posts. It's your introduction to the world—a snapshot of who you are as a writer and what you bring to the table. Whether you're pitching to an editor, a brand, or a potential collaborator, your portfolio is your chance to say, "This is why you should trust me to tell your story."

Start Small, Start Local

You don't need to have travelled the globe to start building your portfolio. Some of my best early pieces came from writing about places I knew intimately. For example, I wrote a piece about Birmingham's seafood market, capturing the lively energy and characters that make it special. "The air smelled of salt and freshly shucked oysters, while the chatter of traders competed with the clatter of crates being loaded onto vans. It wasn't just a market—it was a theatre of life, gritty and unapologetically real."

Writing about local experiences not only helps you hone your craft but also shows editors and brands that you can find compelling stories anywhere—even in the everyday.

Diversity is Key

A strong portfolio demonstrates range. It's one thing to write a glowing review of a luxury hotel; it's another to capture the raw, chaotic beauty of a street market or the quiet charm of a hidden café.

When curating your portfolio, aim to include pieces that reflect different styles, tones, and topics. For instance:

- **Destination Features**: Paint a vivid picture of a place, from its landmarks to its hidden gems.
- **Personal Narratives**: Share a story that's deeply personal but universally relatable.
- **Cultural Deep Dives**: Explore the history, traditions, or quirks that make a destination unique.
- **Practical Guides**: Write a "how-to" piece that's informative and engaging, like a weekend itinerary or tips for navigating public transport.

Each piece should highlight a different aspect of your skills, showing that you can adapt your writing to suit various audiences and formats.

Polish Your Best Work

It's tempting to include everything you've ever written in your portfolio, but less is more. Focus on quality over quantity. A handful of exceptional pieces will do far more for your credibility than a dozen mediocre ones.

Take the time to edit and refine each piece before adding it to your portfolio. Ask yourself:

- Is the story engaging from start to finish?
- Does it reflect my voice and perspective?
- Is it free of typos and grammatical errors?

If you're not confident in your editing skills, consider hiring a professional editor or asking a trusted friend for feedback. Your portfolio should reflect the best version of your work.

Leverage Digital Platforms

In today's world, your portfolio needs to be online. A simple website or blog is an excellent way to showcase your work, but platforms like Medium, Substack, or even LinkedIn can also be effective. The goal is to make it easy for potential collaborators to find and browse your work.

When creating your online portfolio, keep it clean and user-friendly. Organise your pieces by category or destination, and include a brief introduction that tells visitors who you are and what you do. Think of it as your digital calling card—simple, polished, and professional.

Pitch, Publish, and Build

One of the most effective ways to grow your portfolio is to pitch your work to established publications. Start small, with niche travel websites or local magazines. Once you've built up a few bylines, you can begin pitching to larger outlets.

When pitching, tailor your ideas to the publication. Editors appreciate pitches that show you understand their audience and style. For example, if you're pitching to a family travel blog, focus on kid-friendly destinations or activities. If you're pitching to a luxury magazine, highlight high-end experiences like boutique hotels or fine dining.

Every new byline strengthens your portfolio, adding credibility and reach.

Collaborations and Side Projects

Building a portfolio isn't just about solo writing—it's also about collaboration. Partnering with photographers, videographers, or other writers can add depth and diversity to your work. For instance, I once collaborated with a photographer for a piece on Edinburgh's Fringe Festival. Their images brought my words to life, and the final product was far stronger than anything I could have created alone.

Side projects can also be a valuable addition to your portfolio. If you've started a travel blog, hosted a podcast, or created a YouTube channel, showcase these projects as part of your body of work. They demonstrate initiative, creativity, and the ability to connect with an audience.

Keep It Updated

Your portfolio isn't static—it's a living, evolving representation of your career. As you publish new pieces, update your portfolio to reflect your latest and greatest work. Remove older pieces that no longer represent your style or skills.

Think of your portfolio as a garden: it needs regular pruning and care to thrive.

Your Portfolio as a Story

Ultimately, your portfolio isn't just a collection of writing—it's a story about who you are as a writer. Each piece should contribute to a cohesive narrative, one that showcases your passions, your voice, and your ability to connect with readers.

So start small. Start local. And let your portfolio grow, piece by piece, into a body of work that reflects the journey you've taken—and the journey you're inviting others to join.

Chapter 10: Monetising Your Work

Travel writing is a labour of love, but let's not ignore the obvious—it's also a potential source of income. Turning your passion into a sustainable career requires more than just a knack for storytelling; it demands strategy, creativity, and a willingness to diversify your income streams. In this chapter, I'll share the practical ways you can monetise your work, from traditional avenues like publishing to modern platforms like Patreon.

The first rule of marketing your brand is simple: stay true to yourself. Readers can sense when someone is being disingenuous, and nothing kills engagement faster than inauthenticity. Share your real experiences, opinions, and quirks—they're what make your brand memorable.

When I wrote about my visit to London's South Bank, I didn't try to sound overly polished or formal. Instead, I leaned into the candid, conversational tone that readers expect from me: "The South Bank is London at its most unapologetically eclectic—street performers juggling fire, couples sipping overpriced lattes, and me, trying not to drop my camera into the Thames while snapping the perfect shot of the Eye."

1. Writing Books and Ebooks

Publishing your own book is one of the most rewarding ways to establish authority and generate income as a travel writer. Whether it's a memoir, a guidebook, or a collection of travel essays, books allow you to tell longer, richer stories that stand the test of time.

When I began considering writing a travel book, I realised that I didn't need to cover the entire world—just the places where I had the deepest insights. For example, writing about London's South Bank or

Birmingham's seafood market allowed me to lean into my personal experiences and create something unique.

Self-publishing platforms like Amazon Kindle Direct Publishing (KDP) have made it easier than ever to produce and distribute your own book. The key is to find a niche—whether it's urban travel, off-the-beaten-path adventures, or food tourism—and tailor your book to that audience.

Ebooks are a fantastic way to supplement your income. They're quick to produce, require minimal overhead, and can be marketed directly to your audience. Consider creating downloadable itineraries, how-to guides, or niche travel tips. For example, "A Weekend in Edinburgh: Hidden Gems and Local Favourites" could be a perfect ebook for travellers planning a short trip.

2. Blogging for Revenue

Blogs remain one of the most accessible ways to monetise travel writing. If you're consistent and strategic, a well-maintained blog can become a reliable source of income.

Here's how to make blogging work for you:

- **Affiliate Marketing**: Partner with companies like Amazon or Booking.com to earn a commission whenever someone books through your links. For instance, if you're writing about the best places to stay in Edinburgh, include affiliate links to recommended hotels.

- **Sponsored Posts**: As your blog grows, brands may approach you to write about their products, services, or destinations. Just be sure to disclose sponsorships transparently to maintain credibility.

- **Ad Revenue**: Platforms like Google AdSense allow you to display ads on your blog, earning money based on clicks or impressions. While this won't make you rich overnight, it can be a steady supplemental income.

To succeed as a blogger, focus on SEO (Search Engine Optimisation). Use targeted keywords, write engaging headlines, and create content that answers specific questions or solves problems for readers.

3. Collaborating with Brands

Brands and tourism boards are always on the lookout for authentic voices to promote their offerings. As a travel writer, you can collaborate with them in several ways:

- **Press Trips**: Many tourism boards invite writers to experience their destinations in exchange for coverage.

- **Social Media Partnerships**: If you have a strong presence on platforms like Instagram or Twitter, brands may pay you to share sponsored posts.

- **Content Creation**: Some companies hire travel writers to create blogs, social media content, or promotional materials for their own platforms.

When pitching to brands, focus on what you can offer. Highlight your audience demographics, engagement rates, and the unique value of your perspective. Remember, brands are investing in your ability to tell stories that resonate—not just your ability to sell.

4. Patreon and Subscription Platforms

Platforms like Patreon allow you to create exclusive content for your most loyal fans. This can include:

- Behind-the-scenes travel stories
- In-depth guides and itineraries
- Exclusive photos and videos

- Monthly Q&A sessions or webinars

The key to success on Patreon is to offer value that readers can't find anywhere else. For instance, you could share your personal tips for navigating London's markets or create a series of in-depth posts about Edinburgh's hidden gems.

5. Writing for Magazines and Online Publications

Freelance writing remains one of the most traditional—and respected—ways to monetise your work. Pitching articles to magazines, newspapers, or high-traffic websites can not only earn you income but also elevate your profile as a writer.

To increase your chances of success:

- Tailor your pitch to the publication's audience and style.
- Offer a unique angle or perspective.
- Provide a portfolio link to showcase your previous work.

Even if freelance gigs aren't your primary focus, they're an excellent way to build credibility and reach new readers.

6. Teaching and Consulting

As you gain experience, you may find opportunities to teach others about travel writing. This could include:

- Hosting workshops or webinars
- Offering one-on-one coaching sessions
- Writing and selling online courses

Position yourself as an expert, and you'll be surprised at how many aspiring writers are willing to pay for your insights.

7. Diversify and Adapt

The most successful travel writers don't rely on a single income stream—they diversify. By combining books, blogs, collaborations, and other revenue sources, you can create a steady income that's resilient to changes in the industry.

For example, if affiliate revenue from your blog slows down, you might focus on growing your Patreon. If brand collaborations dry up, you could pitch more freelance articles. Flexibility is key.

Making Monetisation Work for You

At its core, monetising your travel writing isn't about chasing every opportunity—it's about finding the ones that align with your skills, interests, and long-term goals. Not every writer wants to manage a blog or teach workshops, and that's okay. Choose the paths that excite you and focus your energy there.

With a thoughtful approach and a willingness to experiment, you can turn your love of travel writing into a career that's both creatively fulfilling and financially sustainable.

Chapter 11: Marketing Your Brand

In the world of travel writing, you are the brand. Your stories, your voice, your experiences—they're what set you apart in a sea of travel content. Marketing your brand isn't about creating a persona or selling an illusion; it's about amplifying what makes you unique. The goal is to build a loyal audience that trusts your perspective, engages with your work, and looks forward to every piece you create.

Mastering Social Media

Social media is one of the most powerful tools for building your brand. Platforms like Instagram, Twitter, and TikTok allow you to reach a global audience, showcase your personality, and connect directly with your readers.

- **Instagram**: Focus on high-quality visuals paired with compelling captions. Use Stories to share behind-the-scenes moments and Reels for quick, engaging content. For example, a Reel of the bustling seafood market in Birmingham could pair quick cuts of fresh fish, lively traders, and your own reactions.

- **Twitter**: Perfect for sharing bite-sized observations, engaging in travel conversations, and promoting your latest pieces. Use hashtags like #TravelTuesday or #Wanderlust to increase visibility.

- **TikTok**: Embrace the short-form video trend by creating quick, punchy clips that highlight unique moments from your travels. Think: "Five Hidden Gems in Edinburgh" or "How to Master the Tube Like a Londoner."

- **Engagement Matters**: Reply to comments, ask questions, and start conversations. Social media isn't just about broadcasting—it's about building a community.

SEO: Making Your Content Discoverable

If you're running a blog or website, Search Engine Optimisation (SEO) is non-negotiable. SEO ensures that your content ranks high on search engines, making it easier for readers to find you.

- **Use Keywords Strategically**: Identify the terms your target audience is searching for and incorporate them naturally into your posts. For example, if you're writing about Princes Street, include phrases like "best things to do on Princes Street" or "hidden gems near Princes Street."

- **Write Descriptive Titles and Meta Descriptions**: These are the first things readers see in search results, so make them enticing and informative.

- **Focus on Long-Form Content**: In-depth guides and essays tend **Optimise Images**: Use descriptive filenames and alt text to improve search visibility.

SEO might seem technical, but it's one of the best ways to ensure your work reaches a wider audience.

The Power of Email Newsletters

While social media gets the spotlight, email newsletters are an underrated powerhouse for building a dedicated audience. Unlike social media, where algorithms control who sees your content, email gives you direct access to your readers.

Use newsletters to:

- Share your latest posts or projects.
- Offer exclusive travel tips, itineraries, or behind-the-scenes stories.
- Connect with your audience on a personal level.

Keep your tone conversational, and don't overdo the self-promotion. A simple, engaging newsletter can build loyalty and keep readers coming back for more.

Collaborate to Grow

Partnerships can be a game-changer when marketing your brand. Collaborate with other travel writers, photographers, or influencers to reach new audiences. Guest blogging, co-hosting webinars, or even joining Instagram Lives can introduce you to potential readers who share your interests.

For example, teaming up with a food blogger to create a guide to Birmingham's best eats could be mutually beneficial, combining your storytelling with their culinary expertise.

Create a Consistent Presence

Consistency is key to building a strong brand. Use the same profile picture, handle, and bio across all platforms to make yourself easily recognisable. Develop a content calendar to ensure you're posting regularly, whether it's weekly blog updates, daily Instagram posts, or monthly newsletters.

At the same time, consistency doesn't mean monotony. Experiment with new formats, styles, and topics to keep your audience engaged.

Sell the Idea of You

Ultimately, marketing your brand is about selling *you*. Your voice, your experiences, your perspective—that's what makes your work valuable. Be bold in showcasing your personality. If you love dry humour, let it shine in your captions. If you're a sucker for hidden gems, make that your niche.

When I wrote about the London Eye, I didn't just describe the view; I shared how it made me feel: "There's something humbling about seeing London spread out beneath you—its history, its chaos, its charm—all from the quiet perch of a glass capsule. For a few minutes, you're part of something bigger, yet somehow, it feels entirely your own."

This personal touch is what draws readers in and keeps them coming back.

Authenticity Over Perfection

Finally, remember that marketing isn't about perfection. It's about connection. Readers don't want a flawless version of you; they want the real you—messy moments, honest reflections, and all. Embrace your quirks, share your mishaps, and let your authenticity shine.

Because at the end of the day, your brand isn't just about the places you've been—it's about the person who's been there.

Chapter 12: Be Authentic, Be You

If there's one lesson I've learned in my years as a travel writer, it's this: authenticity isn't just a buzzword—it's the foundation of your brand. In a world overflowing with perfectly curated content, what sets you apart isn't how flawless your photos are or how many stamps you have in your passport. It's your voice, your quirks, and your unapologetic honesty about the journey—both literal and figurative.

Let's get one thing straight: if marketing your brand feels like a chore, you're doing it wrong. The moment you start forcing yourself to churn out content just to keep up with the algorithm is the moment your work loses its soul. Writing should feel like an extension of your curiosity, a natural expression of the world as you see it. If you're not feeling it, then pause. Take a step back. Recharge. Because the rule number zero of any writing—be it a travel article, a blog post, or a tweet—is that it should feel genuine.

The Laws of Authenticity

These are guiding principles to help you keep your work rooted in who you are while navigating the ever-shifting landscape of social media and audience expectations.

1. The Law of Voice:

Your voice is your superpower. It's what makes your writing recognisable and, more importantly, relatable. Think of it as the fingerprint of your brand—entirely unique to you. My writing voice is conversational, sometimes self-deprecating, and always curious. When I wrote about London's South Bank, I didn't try to sound like a polished journalist:

"The South Bank is London at its most unapologetically eclectic—street performers juggling fire, couples sipping overpriced lattes, and me, trying not to drop my camera into the Thames while snapping the perfect shot of the Eye."

That line worked because it was true to how I experienced the moment. Your voice should feel the same way—unfiltered, unmistakably yours.

2. The Law of Flow:

Your writing doesn't always have to be consistent. One piece might feel whimsical and poetic; another might lean into sharp, observational humour. That's okay. Authenticity isn't about sticking to a single tone—it's about reflecting the multifaceted ways you experience the world.

Think of your brand as a playlist, not a single track. Sometimes you need a ballad; other times, a dance anthem. As long as the core—your voice—remains true, your readers will follow the rhythm.

3. The Law of Resonance:

Great writing isn't just about what you want to say; it's about what your audience needs to hear. This doesn't mean pandering—it means understanding how your experiences and insights can resonate with others.

When I wrote about my misadventures in Istanbul's maze of streets, I focused less on the landmarks and more on the universal experience of being lost and frustrated in a foreign city. The result? A story that readers found funny, relatable, and memorable.

Adapting in the Age of Short Attention Spans

Let's talk about the elephant in the room: social media. Platforms like Threads, YouTube Shorts, and TikTok have rewired the way people consume content. Attention spans are shorter, scrolling is faster, and audiences expect you to hook them in seconds. This doesn't mean you have to turn your writing into clickbait—but it does mean you need to be intentional about capturing your reader's attention.

Here's my strategy: treat your first sentence like the opening scene of a movie. It needs to grab attention, set the tone, and make your audience want to know what happens next.

For example, instead of starting with "I visited Istanbul last summer," try:

"The taxi driver quoted a price twice what the app displayed, and his shrug told me all I needed to know: take it or leave it."

That line immediately introduces tension, character, and a sense of place—all in fewer than 20 words.

When You Don't Feel Like Writing

Let's be honest: there will be days when writing feels like pulling teeth. Creativity ebbs and flows, and that's perfectly normal. When the ideas just aren't coming, don't force it. Instead, try one of these approaches:

- **Read More:** Immerse yourself in the work of writers you admire. You'll start to absorb their rhythms, their techniques, and their ability to turn the mundane into the magical.

- **Revisit Old Notes:** Dig through your travel journal or camera roll. Sometimes, a forgotten detail—a quirky shopkeeper, a strange dish, a fleeting conversation—can spark a story.

- **Adopt a Framework:** If inspiration is low, lean on structure. Start with a vivid sensory detail, follow with a moment of conflict, and end with a reflection. Frameworks aren't crutches; they're scaffolding for creativity.

Remember, your best work will always come from a place of genuine enthusiasm. If you're not feeling it, step away and let the idea percolate. As I like to say, "Good writing takes time. Great writing takes tea breaks."

Evolving with Your Audience

As you grow as a writer, so will your audience—and their expectations. Staying authentic doesn't mean being static. It means evolving in a way that feels natural.

The more you write, the more you'll develop an intuitive sense of what works. You'll start to feel when a story needs humour, when it calls for reflection, and when it's time to just let the scene speak for itself. This feeling—this writer's instinct—is your greatest asset. Trust it.

The Final Word on Being You

Your authenticity is your brand. It's what makes your work stand out in a sea of perfectly filtered travel photos and cookie-cutter captions. It's what makes readers connect with you, trust you, and come back for more.

So write what you feel. Share what you see. And don't be afraid to let your voice evolve. Because at the end of the day, your brand isn't about perfection—it's about connection.

And that connection? It starts with being unapologetically, unmistakably you.

Your Journey as a Travel Writer

Travel writing is more than a craft—it's a calling. It's about capturing fleeting moments, translating them into stories, and sharing them with the world. Along the way, you'll discover that this journey isn't just about the places you visit or the words you write; it's about the connections you build, the insights you gain, and the growth you experience as a storyteller.

When I look back on my own path, I see a mix of missteps, breakthroughs, and moments of pure magic. From the bustling seafood market in Birmingham to the quiet charm of Princes Street, every experience has taught me something valuable about the world—and about myself. Travel writing forces you to look closer, to ask deeper questions, and to find meaning in the details.

Departing Tips for Aspiring Travel Writers

As you embark on your own journey as a travel writer, here are a few parting tips to guide you:

1. Stay Curious

The best travel writers are endlessly curious. Always ask, "Why?" Why is this place the way it is? Why does this moment feel significant? Your curiosity will lead you to stories that others overlook.

2. Write First, Edit Later

Don't let perfectionism stop you from putting words on the page. Write freely, capturing the essence of the moment, and worry about polishing it later. Sometimes, the best lines come from messy first drafts.

3. Find Your Voice

Your voice is what sets you apart. Embrace your quirks, your humour, your unique perspective. Readers don't just want to see the world—they want to see it through your eyes.

4. Respect the Places You Write About

Travel writing comes with a responsibility to represent places and people honestly and respectfully. Avoid stereotypes and overgeneralisation. Instead, focus on the nuances that make each destination unique.

5. Don't Be Afraid to Evolve

Your style, interests, and goals as a writer will change over time—and that's okay. Embrace the evolution, and let it shape your stories in new and exciting ways.

6. Build Relationships, Not Just an Audience

Engage with your readers, collaborate with other writers, and connect with locals during your travels. The relationships you build will enrich your writing and open doors to new opportunities.

7. Take Risks

The best stories often come from stepping out of your comfort zone. Say yes to the unexpected, explore the unfamiliar, and don't be afraid to fail.

The Next Chapter Awaits

This book is a guide, but it's only the beginning. Your journey as a travel writer will be as unique as the stories you tell. Whether you're writing for yourself, an audience, or both, remember that the act of writing is its own reward. It's a way to make sense of the world, to preserve the moments that matter, and to share a piece of yourself with others.

So pack your notebook, sharpen your pen, and start writing. The world is waiting for your story.